RAND

Private Versus Public Sector Insurance Coverage for Drug Abuse

Jeannette A. Rogowski

Drug Policy Research Center

Preface

This report was prepared under the auspices of the Drug Policy Research Center, with funding from the Ford and Weingart Foundations. It is intended to provide policymakers with information on the mechanisms currently in place to finance treatment for drug abuse, with a particular emphasis on insurance coverage. The report also delineates options available to policymakers to increase the availability and use of treatment services.

A shorter version of this report appeared in *Health Affairs*, Vol. 11, No. 3, Fall 1992, pp. 137–148.

Contents

Figures

Tables

Summary

Because a large number of persons abuse drugs, the policy community has recently focused attention on the need for expanded treatment services. This report examines the financing mechanisms currently in place for drug treatment. It also delineates options available to policymakers to increase the availability and use of treatment services. Although direct financing mechanisms are discussed, the main focus of the report is insurance coverage for drug abuse. Specific attention is paid to the differences between public and private insurance mechanisms.[1]

Private insurance coverage for drug abuse treatment is quite limited. Among employees of medium and large firms, for instance, only slightly more than half of plan participants have coverage for both the detoxification and rehabilitation phases of drug treatment (BLS, 1989). Since smaller firms tend to have less generous health insurance benefits, the overall availability of insurance for drug treatment services in the private sector is even less. Among those with coverage, limitations typically exist on the amount of treatment that can be received per year or per lifetime. Since drug abuse is a chronic, recurring condition, this implies that benefits are easily exhausted.

Public insurance consists of three large programs: Medicaid, Medicare, and CHAMPUS. Medicaid is a program for certain categories of low-income persons, Medicare is for the blind, aged, and disabled, and CHAMPUS is for military retirees (and their dependents) as well as dependents of active duty military. The programs with the most generous benefits—Medicare and CHAMPUS—are also the programs with the most restrictive eligibility requirements. Among public programs, Medicaid has the least generous drug treatment benefits. Its eligibility requirements unfortunately also exclude a large fraction of the drug abusing population. Males between the ages of 22 and 64 are very likely to be excluded from coverage.

The benefit structures of private and public insurance differ considerably. Whereas private plans tend to limit benefits, thereby controlling demand for treatment services, public insurance tends to place restrictions on the providers

---

[1]Insurance coverage reflects the state of benefits in 1990.

of care. Such restrictions typically include limits on the level of payments to providers and the inpatient settings in which care can be received.

Several options are open to policymakers to increase the availability of insurance coverage for drug abuse. On the private side, both federal and state governments have the authority to regulate insurance benefits. These regulations may take the form of either mandated availability of coverage or a mandated minimum benefit package.

On the public side, the most important current constraint on the availability of insurance coverage is the highly restrictive eligibility requirements for public programs. This is particularly true of the Medicaid program, which is designed to provide insurance coverage for low-income persons and is the program one would expect to cover the largest number of drug abusers. Because eligibility is linked to specific welfare programs, such as Aid to Families with Dependent Children (AFDC) and Supplemental Security Income (SSI), increasing eligibility for drug abusers may be quite difficult.

Aside from eligibility constraints, the lack of specific provisions in federal Medicaid guidelines to provide coverage for drug abuse treatment also contributes to a lack of access to treatment among the poor. For instance, states are not required to provide coverage for rehabilitation. Coverage for drug abuse treatment varies by state, often considerably. Federal mandates for the inclusion of drug treatment services in Medicaid would serve to increase access to care.

Coverage provisions under Medicaid for pregnant women are particularly problematic. Whereas all poor pregnant women are automatically eligible for Medicaid, treatment for drug abuse is not necessarily covered. The children born to these mothers have a high risk of being of low birthweight and therefore incurring large medical expenses. Since Medicaid must also provide coverage for the medical care provided to infants born to poor mothers, it would be advisable to expand coverage to include maternal drug treatment services.

Medicaid also places significant restrictions on the types of treatments that can be received. These relate primarily to the settings in which treatment for drug abuse can occur. Two specific provisions in the Medicaid statutes have significant implications for the delivery of medical services to treat drug abuse. The first of these is that Medicaid cannot pay for treatment given in residential settings. The second is that medical care for adults under the age of 65 cannot be provided in institutions for mental disease. Since drug abuse is classified as a mental disease in the international classification of diseases, this excludes care provided in facilities that specialize in the treatment of substance abuse. Since inpatient care can be provided only in the most expensive treatment setting—hospitals—some states, such as California, have chosen to provide virtually no inpatient treatment for drug abuse. The state of Michigan has a different response. It does cover residential treatment facilities, forgoing the federal cost share of 50 percent. As indicated by Medicaid, the interrelationships between state and federal governments are key to the formulation of effective policies to increase the availability of treatment services for drug abuse.

In the current policy debate, some have argued that the public sector should move away from the direct provision of treatment toward the provision of more insurance (Gerstein and Harwood, 1990). The conclusion reached here is that the mainstreaming of drug treatment financing into Medicaid is not likely to occur because of significant institutional barriers.

1. Introduction

Because so many people abuse drugs, attention in the policy community has focused recently on the need for expanded treatment services.[1] The use of treatment services depends on many factors, including recognition by the individual of a need, the ability of the abuser to pay for treatment, and the availability of necessary services. This research concerns itself with the latter two aspects of treatment for drug abuse. The availability and demand for services are themselves a function of existing mechanisms for financing drug abuse treatment. Insurance, by increasing the ability to pay for treatment services, is one way to increase demand for drug abuse treatment. In the current policy debate, some have argued that the public sector should move toward the provision of more insurance for treatment (Gerstein and Harwood, 1990). This report discusses the financing mechanisms currently in place, both through insurance and direct funding, and delineates available policy options to increase the availability and use of treatment services.[2] The conclusion reached here is that the mainstreaming of drug treatment financing into Medicaid is not likely to occur because of significant institutional barriers.

Both the private and public sectors play a large role in the financing of drug abuse treatment. Total drug abuse treatment expenditures in 1990 exceeded $2 billion (ONDCP, 1990). The public sector, however, provides the majority of the funding, accounting for 59 percent of treatment dollars (NDATUS, 1989).[3] In contrast, as indicated in Figure 1, for medical expenditures in general, the public sector accounts for only 41 percent of total expenditures (Letsch et al., 1988). One reason that the public sector plays such a large role in the financing of drug abuse treatment is that a large fraction of treatment expenditures come in the

---

[1]A recent report by the Institute of Medicine estimates that 5.5 million persons "clearly or probably need treatment" (Gerstein and Harwood, 1990).

[2]The sources for this research include published reports, journal articles, insurance manuals, and federal and state regulations. Interviews were also conducted with representatives of private insurance companies, Medicare, Medicaid, the Civilian Health and Medical Programs of the Uniformed Services (CHAMPUS), and state insurance regulatory agencies.

[3]The NDATUS funding service category "other" (which comprised 3 percent of overall expenditures) was included in our category of public expenditures for the purposes of these calculations. Because of underreporting of facilities, both public and private treatment expenditures are likely to be undercounted in NDATUS. Expenditures for drug treatment may also be higher than the figures here suggest because of its potential inclusion in general medical services. For instance, drug treatment that occurs as part of prenatal care for pregnant women may not be counted. See NDATUS (1989).

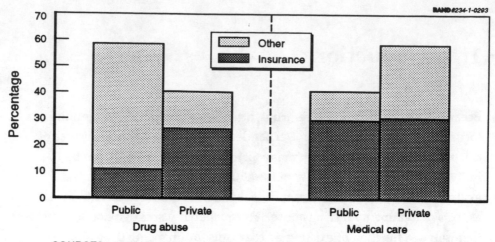

SOURCES: 1987 NDATUS data (1989); Letsch et al. (1988).

Figure 1—Expenditures on Drug Abuse

form of direct treatment dollars from the government, such as federal block grants. In fact, almost half of treatment expenditures come from either these types of grants or other direct support from state and local government programs. These programs typically provide treatment funds directly to providers. Care received by public clients depends on the availability of slots from such providers. Public insurance, which provides treatment on demand, is relatively rare, accounting for only one-fifth of public expenditures and one-tenth of total treatment dollars (NDATUS, 1989). This pattern of financing is in sharp contrast to that for medical care in general, where almost three-quarters of public expenditures are paid by insurance.

Whereas public insurance has a small role in treatment financing, private insurance plays a significant role, accounting for 27 percent of total treatment expenditures (NDATUS, 1989). Two-thirds of private dollars come from insurance.[4] Thus, although the financing of drug abuse treatment is dominated by the public sector, the mix of financing between insurance and other sources varies considerably between the private and public sectors. The private sector is dominated by insurance. The public sector is dominated by direct funding for treatment.

The large volume of direct public subsidies for drug treatment has significant implications for the delivery of treatment services to public clients. In particular, this part of the treatment system is one where care is rationed. The insured part

---

[4]The "private other" category includes, *inter alia*, fees paid directly by clients and copayments paid by those with insurance.

of the treatment system is one where care is received on demand for those with insurance coverage. Since the total number of dollars allocated to treatment services in the public sector is fixed, there is a limit on the number of treatment services that can be provided. These services must therefore be rationed. Rationing should ideally occur in a way that makes the most effective use of existing treatment funds. This is not the case for drug treatment. Rationing occurs primarily through waiting times instead of being based on need. Given excess demand for a limited number of treatment slots, patients must wait in line for their turn for treatment. This is particularly problematic for drug abuse, where it is often difficult for the abuser to recognize that a problem of addiction exists. Once turned away from a treatment slot, he may not return later when one is available.

Furthermore, even if enough slots are available, very little matching of programs to the patient needs occurs. Generally, care is received from the provider the patient seeks out, whether or not that particular provider would be the best match for his needs. Since the patient is not in a position to know which programs suit him best, some sort of gatekeeping mechanism is necessary to ensure an efficient allocation of resources. Some attempts at gatekeeping mechanisms do exist. In the District of Columbia, for instance, there is a central intake point for all public drug abuse clients. They are then referred to the programs deemed most suitable. The client, however, may or may not decide to choose that treatment site, or may choose not to obtain treatment at all.

An alternative to the provision of direct funding for treatment is insurance. Insurance decreases the financial barriers to receiving treatment by reducing the price to the patient. Rationing mechanisms are unnecessary, because insurance coverage creates treatment on demand.[5] From the patient's perspective, this means that waiting for a treatment slot is not necessary. This is evident from the fact that the private sector, which is dominated by insurance, has high vacancy rates, as opposed to the public sector, which is essentially running at capacity (ONDCP, 1990). With insurance coverage, the implicit number of services that can be provided is not capped. From the perspective of policymakers, however, this means that total budgetary outlays for drug treatment cannot be directly controlled.

---

[5]Of course, if the number of providers is too small to meet the demand, then rationing can also occur in the presence of insurance. The evidence from the private sector, however, is that as private insurance for drug abuse became more prevalent, the number of private providers grew to meet the demand (Gerstein and Harwood, 1990). This may not be the case, however, in the public sector because of low payment rates on the part of public insurers.

The provision of insurance coverage, while avoiding rationing, still may not result in a favorable allocation of resources. As in the public treatment system, with insurance little matching of treatments to the need of the patients is made. Patients are triaged into treatment settings by their own choice of providers. They are rarely in a position to judge which sort of treatment is optimal. Thus, in the absence of a mechanism to match patients to treatments, resources may not be allocated efficiently.[6]

Although in theory insurance provides for treatment on demand, in practice this is far from true. In both the private and public sectors, benefits for drug abuse treatment are extremely limited. On the public side, this stems from an effort to control program expenditures; on the private side, it stems from the need to control health insurance premiums. The limitation of benefits by private insurers is due in part to the difficulty of assessing responsiveness to treatment and thus of estimating the total cost and duration of treatment. The "public safety net" provided by block grant funding may also contribute to an unwillingness to provide generous benefits. The private sector controls use by such mechanisms as limiting the number of days of treatment that are covered, creating lifetime limits on the number of episodes for which treatment can be sought, and requiring higher copayments for drug treatment than for other medical services. Given the recurring nature of the need for drug abuse treatment, insurance coverage under such schemes is likely to be quickly exhausted, leaving patients to either pay for treatment out-of-pocket or to wait for a public treatment slot. The public sector controls use by restrictions on providers, such as capping payments to providers on behalf of public beneficiaries and placing restrictions on treatment settings and the types of treatments provided. These restrictions, described in detail below, have significant implications for policymakers' ability to mainstream drug treatment financing away from block grant funding and into Medicaid.

This report focuses on insurance coverage for drug abuse. It describes the characteristics of existing types of insurance for drug abuse treatment and the resultant implications for access to and use of services. Specific attention is paid to the differences between public and private insurance mechanisms. Public and private insurance differ markedly, for instance, in the methods used to control the use of services. Whereas private plans tend to control the demand for treatment by benefit limitations, public insurance tends to place restrictions on

---

[6]For employed private patients, the presence of Employee Assistance Programs (EAPs) in the workplace that refer abusers to treatment centers may result in an effective gatekeeping mechanism. Patients with insurance that involves managed care, such as Health Maintenance Organizations, are also subject to gatekeeping mechanisms.

the providers of care. Restrictions on eligibility in the public sector and on benefits in the private sector result in exclusion of coverage for those most in need of treatment. Further, on the public side, low payment levels restrict access to care. However, providers may be able to offset part of this shortfall in revenues by using block grant funding.

Public insurance consists of three large programs: Medicaid, Medicare, and CHAMPUS. Medicaid is a program for certain categories of low-income persons, Medicare is for the blind, aged, and disabled, and CHAMPUS is for military retirees (and their dependents) as well as dependents of active duty military. The programs with the most generous benefits—Medicare and CHAMPUS—are also the programs with the most restrictive eligibility requirements. Among public programs, Medicaid has the least generous drug treatment benefits. Its eligibility requirements unfortunately also exclude a large fraction of the drug abusing population.

The remainder of this report focuses on options open to policymakers to increase the availability and types of insurance coverage provided for drug abuse treatment. On the private side, these include the regulation of insurance benefits by both federal and state governments. On the public side, existing institutional barriers may be important determinants of potential changes to the mix of financing. These include highly restrictive eligibility requirements for public insurance programs, and specific exclusions in the types of treatments that can be provided by public insurers. Finally, the complementary, and sometimes conflicting roles of state and federal governments in the financing of drug treatment services will be analyzed. These interrelationships are particularly evident in the Medicaid program. The federal government sets the general guidelines for Medicaid benefits and enforces certain exclusions, such as care in residential treatment facilities. States, on the other hand, have great latitude in interpreting the federal guidelines and may provide benefits for drug abuse treatment that are more or less generous. States may also choose to override specific federal exclusions, such as care in residential treatment facilities, by forgoing the federal cost share of those services, which is a minimum of 50 percent. They may also extend eligibility to a wider range of low-income persons, again forgoing the federal cost share for those not eligible under federal guidelines.

This discussion should provide a comprehensive view of the current system of financing for drug abuse treatment[7] through insurance as well as options for change given existing institutional arrangements.

---

[7]The benefit structures described for public programs are those in effect in 1990.

2. Private Insurance

Insurance in the private sector is primarily obtained through the employment relation. In 1987, two-thirds of the U.S. population was covered by employment-related health insurance (Short et al., 1989). A knowledge of the extent and types of coverages provided by private health insurance policies for drug abuse is therefore important to an understanding of the availability of insurance for drug abuse treatment. The number of employed persons with coverage for drug abuse treatment is limited. Furthermore, private policies, if they do provide benefits for drug abuse treatment, tend to tightly limit the amount of treatment that can be received. Since drug abuse is a chronic recurring condition, benefits are likely to be exhausted under a typical private policy.

Benefits for Drug Abuse Treatment

Among policies that provide coverage for drug abuse treatment, benefits are generally quite limited. Limits are placed on the amount of care that can be obtained per year and often per lifetime. The typical inpatient treatment package is based on a standard 28-day regimen, providing 7 days of coverage for detoxification and 21 days for rehabilitation. In a 1988 study by Foster Higgins of employer-provided health care plans (Foster Higgins, 1988), 49 percent of plans with a separate drug abuse benefit placed a limit on the number of days per confinement, and 42 percent placed limits on the number of confinements per lifetime.[1] One-quarter of plans limit the dollar amounts payable per lifetime for inpatient care. Outpatient visits in private plans are constrained as well, usually to 20 or 30 visits. In the Foster Higgins study, 37 percent of plans placed limits on the number of visits per year and 47 percent placed limits on the dollar amounts per year. One-quarter of plans placed maximum dollar amounts per lifetime on outpatient care.

Since drug abuse is a chronic, recurring condition, yearly and lifetime limits on coverage imply that drug abusers are likely to exhaust benefits. For instance, 62 percent of employers in the Foster Higgins study that handle mental health and substance abuse separately cover 30 days or less per confinement. Forty-eight

---

[1] The unit of analysis in the Foster Higgins study is the modal health care plan as opposed to the BLS study which includes all health care plans.

percent of these employers limit the number of confinements per year or per lifetime (in most cases to two).[2]

Thus, insurance benefits do not seem to be tailored to the chronic, recurrent nature of drug abuse. In particular, a significant number of drug abusers require more than two episodes of treatment. In the 1985 CODAP study (NIDA, 1985), which collected detailed data on treatment clients, 60 percent of clients had one or more prior episodes of treatment; 40 percent had two or more. Since the CODAP study counts only the number of episodes of care to date, and not per lifetime, lifetime episodes are likely to be even more numerous. Thus, lifetime limits of two episodes of treatment will likely result in an exhaustion of benefits for many drug abusers.

Furthermore, on the inpatient hospital side, a uniform, standard 28-day regimen may not be well suited to the drug treatment needs of all patients. It may provide too little inpatient coverage for some patients and too much for others. At the very least, a few patients have complications either from psychiatric or other problems and are likely to require longer stays. Other patients may have shorter lengths of stay. Data from the CHAMPUS program indicate that current patterns of inpatient hospital care for substance abuse imply a length of stay of considerably less than 28 days for most adults. The average hospital length of stay for substance abuse treatment for adults is 15 days.[3] Conversely, 5 percent of hospital stays exceeded 37 days (*Federal Register*, October 10, 1989). Although the adult population in CHAMPUS may not be representative of the adult population in general (adults in the program are military retirees and their dependents, and dependents of active duty military), this does provide some evidence that currently most adults tend to spend less than 28 days in inpatient treatment and a few require more than 28 days.[4] Thus, providing one uniform benefit for all drug abusers provides too much coverage for some and too little for others. To properly assess whether coverage limitations are inadequate, however, these limitations would have to be compared to effectiveness standards. Unfortunately such standards do not exist for the treatment of drug abuse.

In addition to the limitations described above, private plans typically impose higher copayments for outpatient drug abuse treatment as well. Higher

---

[2]On the outpatient side, 47 percent have a maximum dollar amount per year and 37 percent have a maximum number of visits per year.

[3]This is the average length of stay in diagnosis-related group (DRG) 900.

[4]These numbers represent actual use patterns and make no inferences as to the appropriateness of the length of stay.

outpatient copayments are observed for mental health services in general. Whereas the copayment for medical care is generally 20 percent, among plans that place restrictions, copayments for outpatient drug abuse treatment are typically 50 percent (Foster Higgins, 1988). Higher cost sharing decreases the probability that treatment will be sought (Manning et al., 1988). For drug abuse, this is particularly problematic. It is difficult for abusers to admit that they have a problem and need treatment. Creating financial disincentives will serve only to further discourage persons from seeking treatment. On the private side, out-of-pocket copayments and lifetime benefit limitations are likely to be the most important factors in decreasing demand for treatment.

Who Has Insurance for Drug Abuse Treatment?

The availability of private insurance benefits for drug abuse is a recent phenomenon. The Bureau of Labor Statistics conducts an annual survey of health insurance benefits provided by medium and large firms. These are firms with 100 or more employees. In 1982, only 37 percent of plan participants[5] had a separately defined benefit for drug abuse treatment. By 1984, 52 percent had coverage and in 1986, 66 percent had some separately defined drug abuse treatment benefits. By 1988, the number had risen to 74 percent (BLS, 1989).[6] Recent estimates, based on 1989 data, indicate that 96 percent of health plan enrollees have some form of coverage for drug abuse (Kronson, 1991).[7] Since most plans provide for detoxification under the general medical benefit, however, the apparently high percentage of persons with treatment benefits may be misleading. Drug abuse treatment usually has two phases. The first phase of treatment is detoxification where the patient undergoes withdrawal from the chemical dependency. This is considered a medical phase of treatment and is more likely to be covered than the second phase of treatment, rehabilitation. Rehabilitation is a psychosocial treatment and is less likely to be covered by insurers. In 1988, only slightly more than half of all plan participants had coverage for rehabilitation.[8]

---

[5]A plan participant is a worker covered by a benefit plan and whose employer contributes to the cost of the plan.

[6]In 1988, the study was representative of 31.1 million full-time employees in private, nonagricultural industries. Ninety percent of workers had some form of health insurance.

[7]In 1989, the survey instrument permitted better measurement of inpatient detoxification services. Thus, the large increase observed between 1988 and 1989 is due not only to an increase in the availability of the benefit, but also to better measurement of benefit availability.

[8]Note that plan participants who have drug abuse coverage under their mental health benefit are included in these figures.

These statistics are likely to overestimate the number of persons with employment-related drug abuse coverage, however. Medium and large firms—the firms included in the BLS survey—are those with 100 or more employees. These are the firms most likely to provide health insurance to their employees and to have generous coverage. Smaller firms are much less likely to provide health insurance to their employees and those that do tend to have less generous coverage. Lack of health insurance coverage in firms with 10 workers or less created one-third of the uninsured population in 1987. An additional 25 percent of the uninsured were from firms of 10 to 100 employees (Short et al., 1989). Whereas almost 90 percent of workers and dependents associated with firms of 100 or more have employment-related coverage, only 56.5 percent of workers and dependents in establishments of 10 workers or less have health insurance provided by their employer (Short et al., 1989). Furthermore, only 60 percent of part-time workers and 55 percent of self-employed workers have health insurance coverage (Short et al., 1989). Thus, the number of employed persons with coverage for drug abuse treatment is considerably less than indicated by the statistics mentioned above for medium and large firms. Additionally, drug abusers tend to be young. Young adults between the ages of 19 and 24 are particularly likely to be uninsured. Only half of persons in this age bracket are covered by insurance through an employer or union (Short et al., 1989). Thus, private coverage for drug abuse is particularly lacking in the age brackets most likely to abuse drugs.

State, local, and federal governments are also large employers and are excluded from the BLS study of medium and large firms. Compared to private employers, government appears to have more generous coverage for drug abuse. In a 1987 study of employee benefits in state and local government by the Bureau of Labor Statistics,[9] 94 percent of plan participants had drug abuse coverage for inpatient hospital care and 81 percent had coverage for outpatient care (BLS, 1988).[10] In the federal employees health benefit program in 1990, all of the fee-for-service plans have some coverage for drug abuse treatment (U.S. OPM, 1990).

In summary, then, the number of persons with employer-provided insurance coverage for drug abuse is limited. Among the private plans that do cover drug abuse treatment, benefits are tightly limited. These limitations, combined with the fact that drug abuse is a chronic, recurrent condition, cause insurance benefits to be easily exhausted.

---

[9]The study is representative of 10.3 million full-time employees. Ninety-four percent of workers had some form of health insurance.

[10]Note that outpatient care under BLS definitions includes treatment in residential treatment facilities as previously described.

3. Public Insurance

Public insurance accounts for only 10 percent of overall drug treatment expenditures, primarily because of the highly restrictive eligibility requirements for public programs, which systematically exclude the majority of drug abusers. In addition, among public treatment clients who have insurance coverage, benefits are quite limited. In contrast to the private sector, however, restrictions tend to be placed on the provider rather than on the beneficiary. Thus, instead of trying to influence the demand for treatment services, public insurance programs aim to control the quantity of treatment services provided to those who seek treatment and the settings in which care may be received.

Of the three public insurance programs—Medicaid, Medicare, and CHAMPUS— Medicare is the largest program with 33 million beneficiaries and $81.2 billion in benefit payments in 1987 (HCFA, 1989). Medicaid is the second largest with 23 million recipients and $49.4 billion in benefit payments in 1987 (HCFA, 1989). CHAMPUS is the smallest with approximately 6 million beneficiaries and $2.2 billion in medical benefits in 1988.[1] Yet, despite the large sizes of these programs, expenditures for drug abuse are small. It is estimated that Medicare spent only $50 million on drug abuse treatment and Medicaid $120 million in 1990 (ONDCP, 1990).[2] By contrast, CHAMPUS spent an estimated $32 million on drug abuse treatment in 1988.[3] In 1989, residential treatment for adolescents alone accounted for $110 million in program expenditures. This includes treatment for mental conditions as well as substance abuse. The CHAMPUS program, therefore, although small, constitutes an important fraction of public insurance dollars. Medicare and Medicaid have such small program expenditures because their eligibility requirements systematically exclude the majority of drug abusers. Furthermore, whereas Medicare has fairly generous benefits for drug abuse treatment, Medicaid does not.

---

[1]These figures are unpublished and were provided by the CHAMPUS central office.

[2]Because of data limitations, Medicaid program expenditures for drug abuse are extremely difficult to estimate.

[3]Total mental health expenditures in 1988 were also large, approximately $530 million. Mental health and drug abuse treatment account for such a large fraction of program expenditures because military facilities generally do not provide such treatments. The vast majority of treatment services must be sought in the civilian sector. CHAMPUS provides insurance coverage for care that is not provided in military facilities.

Eligibility

The Medicaid program, designed to provide health insurance to low-income individuals, is the program one might expect to provide the most coverage for drug abusers. Eligibility for Medicaid, however, is generally linked to the welfare system. To be eligible for Medicaid a person must be eligible either for Supplemental Security Income (SSI) or Aid to Families with Dependent Children (AFDC). The only major exception to these rules is that poor pregnant women are also Medicaid-eligible. Aside from pregnancy, to be eligible, a person must be either blind, disabled, aged, or a member of a family with dependent children. These families are defined as those for whom one parent is absent, incapacitated, or dead. These are primarily young females and their dependent children. One group most likely to be excluded from Medicaid coverage are males between the ages of 22 and 64. Most drug abusers are male, however. As indicated in Figure 2, approximately 67 percent of persons in treatment for drug abuse are males and only 33 percent females (NDATUS, 1989).[4] Furthermore, as shown in Figure 3, 77 percent of drug abusers in treatment are between the ages of 20 and 64. Thus, a large part of the poor population that abuses drugs is not eligible for Medicaid. Furthermore, among those with coverage, benefits for drug abuse treatment are not generous.

Eligibility for the Medicare program is linked to the social security system. Persons over the age of 65 or disabled (eligible for SSI) and eligible to receive social security cash payments are eligible for Medicare. Ninety percent of Medicare beneficiaries are over the age of 65. As indicated in Figure 3, only half of one percent of all drug abusers in treatment are over 65 years of age (NDATUS, 1989). Since it is the young population that abuses drugs, the Medicare program eligibility requirements essentially preclude most drug abusers. Young, disabled persons who have worked long enough to become eligible for social security benefits are eligible for Medicare. They currently account for approximately 10 percent of Medicare beneficiaries (3 million persons). Approximately one-third of the disabled[5] in 1987 were under the age of 44, the age bracket in which drug abuse is most prevalent. Furthermore, the number of young beneficiaries has been increasing over time. In 1975, 11.6 percent of the disabled were under the age of 35; this had risen to 15 percent by 1987. Similarly, in 1975, 12 percent of the disabled were between the ages of 35

---

[4]Note that these figures include only persons in treatment and may not necessarily reflect the population in need of treatment.

[5]The disabled are defined as SSI beneficiaries. They are eligible for Medicare only if they have worked long enough to be eligible for social security. Otherwise, if they meet state income requirements they are eligible for Medicaid.

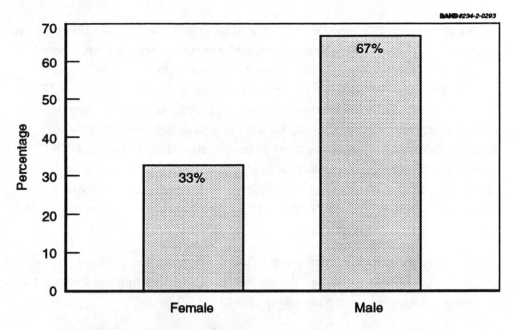

SOURCE: 1987 NDATUS data (1989).

Figure 2—Gender Differences Among Drug Abusers in Treatment

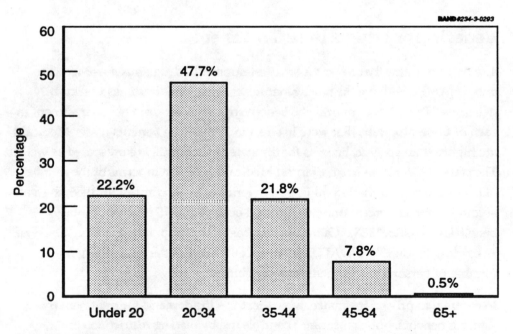

SOURCE: 1987 NDATUS data (1989).

Figure 3—Age Distribution of Drug Abusers in Treatment

and 44; this rose to 18 percent by 1987 (Social Security Bulletin, 1986, 1989). Thus, an increasing number of Medicare beneficiaries are in the age brackets where drug abuse is most prevalent. The number of persons who are classified as disabled because of drug abuse or alcoholism is very small, however, only 17,000 in 1989.[6] This number has increased by a factor of four since 1985, when only 4,000 persons were classified as disabled because of drug abuse or alcoholism. To be so classified, the addiction must be the primary cause of the disability. These persons are required to "accept appropriate treatment, if available, in an approved facility and demonstrate compliance with conditions and requirements for treatment" (Social Security Bulletin, 1986). In addition, SSI payments must be made to a representative payee.

Eligibility for the CHAMPUS program is linked to employment in the military and is therefore quite restrictive. Dependents of active duty military and military retirees and their dependents are eligible for CHAMPUS.

Thus, eligibility requirements for Medicare and Medicaid, the two large programs of public insurance, essentially exclude most of the drug abusing population. The CHAMPUS program, by its very nature, is not one that can provide a broad base of coverage.

Benefits for Drug Abuse Treatment

The two programs that cover the smallest number of drug abusers—Medicare and CHAMPUS—have the most generous benefits. Medicaid has the least generous. Table 1 summarizes the benefit structures for drug abuse treatment in each of these programs that were in effect in 1990. Since benefits under Medicaid are highly state-specific, benefits for the state of California are presented as well. The state of California has the largest Medicaid program in terms of the number of beneficiaries and the second largest in terms of expenditures. In 1986, the state accounted for 11 percent of total Medicaid outlays and 15 percent of total beneficiaries (CRS, 1988). California also has a large population of drug abusers. According to the 1987 NDATUS survey, California has the second largest number of persons in treatment for drug abuse.

In contrast to private insurance, which restricts the demand for treatment by limiting benefits, public insurance controls use by placing restrictions on

---

[6]These unpublished figures were provided by the Social Security Administration.

Table 1

Public Benefit Structures for Drug Abuse Treatment

	Medicaid	California Medicaid	Medicare	CHAMPUS
Coverage by treatment setting				
Inpatient hospital				
General hospital	Yes[a]	Yes[a]	Yes	Yes
Psychiatric hospital	No[b]	No	Yes	Yes
Substance abuse hospital	No	No	Yes	Yes
Residential treatment facility	No	No	No	Yes
Outpatient care	Yes[a]	Yes	Yes	Yes
Limitations on amount of care per treatment episode				
Inpatient hospital	S[c]	(d)	Yes	Yes
Residential treatment facility	N/A	N/A	N/A	Yes
Outpatient care	S	(e)	No	Yes
Limitations on the number of episodes of treatment	No	No	No	No[f]
Cost-sharing				
Separate copayment or deductible	No	No	No[g]	No

[a]Mandatory only if medically necessary.

[b]Care in a psychiatric hospital for persons under the age of 21 may be provided at state option.

[c]S = at the discretion of the state.

[d]Only medically necessary detoxification.

[e]Only 21 days of heroin detoxification.

[f]Under the CHAMPUS alcohol benefit, the limit is three episodes of treatment per lifetime. Under the mental health benefit, there is no limit.

[g]Copayment rate for physician claims not made on assignment is higher (50 percent versus 20 percent).

providers of service. These include restrictions on the settings in which treatment may be provided, on the types of treatments that are covered, and on payments to providers. The latter is the subject of the next section. As indicated in Table 1, all public programs cover outpatient care. Inpatient care, however, is quite restricted. There are two types of inpatient settings for drug abuse treatment: hospitals and residential treatment facilities. The vast majority of hospitals are acute care general hospitals. Some hospitals, however, specialize in the treatment of substance abuse and others specialize in the treatment of persons with psychiatric conditions. Drug abusers are treated in all three types of hospitals. Those with complicating psychiatric conditions or who are severely ill are most likely to be treated in specialized facilities. Figure 4 shows the types of inpatient settings in which treatment is provided.

16

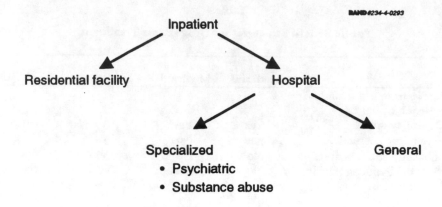

Figure 4—Inpatient Settings for Drug Abuse Treatment

Residential care is the least costly setting in terms of the daily cost of treatment. Hospitals are very expensive because of the high overhead costs of the services they make available to patients. Yet, in the absence of a complicating medical condition, drug abuse treatment rarely makes use of these services. Treatment for drug abuse has two phases—detoxification and rehabilitation. Although detoxification may warrant care in a medical facility, the rehabilitative phase of treatment is a psychosocial one and does not make use of the many medical services available in a hospital. For cases not requiring hospitalization, inpatient care could be provided in other inpatient settings, such as residential facilities, at considerably less expense. Yet, neither Medicare nor Medicaid will pay for inpatient care provided in a residential treatment facility. Both programs, however, will pay for inpatient care in a general hospital. Thus, inpatient care can be provided only in the most expensive treatment setting. This restriction has resulted in differing reactions among states. Michigan does cover residential treatment facilities under its Medicaid program. Because it is excluded under Medicaid, the state does not receive any matching federal dollars for care, which pays for 50 percent of expenses. Yet, residential treatment facilities are so much less expensive than hospitals that the state is willing to forgo the 50 percent federal share.[7] California, on the other hand, does not provide care in residential treatment facilities. It also will not pay for hospital care unless medically necessary. Thus, only medically necessary detoxification in a hospital is covered.

---

[7]This statement is based on conversations with members of the Michigan Department of Health.

The rehabilitation phase is not covered. This means that inpatient care under the California Medicaid program is virtually nonexistent.

The Medicaid program has further restrictions that prevent drug abuse treatment from being provided in specialty hospitals, such as substance abuse or psychiatric hospitals. Although this restriction does not affect the majority of drug abusers, whose treatment needs can be met in other settings, it does affect those who are dually diagnosed or severely ill and in need of treatment in specialized facilities. The institution for mental disease (IMD) exclusion under Medicaid prohibits care from being provided to any person between the ages of 22 and 64 in an institution with more than 16 beds "that is primarily engaged in providing diagnosis, treatment or care of persons with mental diseases, including medical attention, nursing care and related services" 42 CFR Sec. 435.1009 (1989).[8] Since drug abuse is classified as a mental condition in the international classification of diseases, all facilities that specialize in drug abuse treatment are excluded. Even if Medicaid provided coverage for residential treatment facilities, care in them would still not be possible because they would likely fall under the IMD exclusion.

Public insurance differs markedly from private insurance in that no limits are placed on the number of episodes of treatment for which care can be sought. Given the chronic, recurring nature of drug abuse, this is a highly desirable feature of public insurance. The exception to this is the CHAMPUS alcohol benefit, which limits care to three episodes per lifetime. Under CHAMPUS, drug abusers may fall under either a mental health benefit or an alcohol benefit depending on whether alcohol abuse is present as a complicating condition. The majority of drug abusers fall under the alcohol benefit, which is a more restrictive benefit.

Public insurance programs do place limits, however, on the amount, and in some cases, the types of care that can be received. As indicated in Table 2, on the inpatient side, both CHAMPUS and Medicare use a reimbursement system based on DRGs. By paying the hospital a fixed amount per hospital stay, this implicitly limits the number of days of hospital care that are covered. The CHAMPUS program further limits the annual number of days of hospital care to 60 per year under the mental health benefit and to 28 days per episode under the alcohol benefit. The Medicaid program requires states to provide care in the hospital setting only when medically necessary. As we have seen, California provides

---

[8]At state option, care in psychiatric hospitals can be provided for persons under the age of 21.

Table 2

Public Payment Mechanisms

	Medicaid	California Medicaid	Medicare	CHAMPUS
Inpatient hospital				
General hospital	S[a]	Fixed per diem	DRG	DRG
Psychiatric hospital	N/A	N/A	Per diem	Per diem
Substance abuse hospital	N/A	N/A	DRG	DRG
Residential treatment facility	N/A	N/A	N/A	Charge-based
Outpatient	S	Fee schedule	Fee schedule	Charge-based

[a]S = at discretion of the state.

coverage only for medically necessary detoxification in the inpatient hospital setting.

On the outpatient side, restrictions exist as well. The California Medicaid program will pay for heroin detoxification only in the outpatient setting. There is a further limit of 21 days of coverage per episode of care.[9] The CHAMPUS program limits outpatient visits to 60 and family visits to 15 per benefit period under its alcohol benefit. There is no limit on the number of outpatient visits under the mental health benefit. Similarly, there is no limit on the number of outpatient visits under Medicare. This is a recent development, however, in effect only since 1990. Before 1988, Medicare would pay a maximum of only $250 toward outpatient care. This was raised to $450 in 1988 and to $1,100 in 1989. The trend toward fewer restrictions is in direct contrast to the trend in the private sector to increasingly limit benefits.

Although Medicare and Medicaid do not pay for care in a residential treatment facility, CHAMPUS does. The same limits that apply to inpatient hospital care also apply to care in a residential treatment facility. CHAMPUS is notable, however, in that there is a special benefit for the treatment of adolescents in residential settings. If medical certification is received that care in a residential treatment facility is required, then unlimited benefits are available. This benefit alone cost CHAMPUS $110 million in 1989 for the care of approximately 3,000 adolescents. The average cost per case was $37,000 with an average length of stay of 249 days.[10] These adolescents were treated primarily for mental illnesses, but a substantial number had a secondary diagnosis of substance abuse. The expenditures for this benefit alone are twice as high as the entire program

---

[9]Four other types of outpatient treatment may be available at the county level through an interagency agreement with the Department of Alcohol and Drug Programs.

[10]Unpublished data from the CHAMPUS central office.

expenditures of Medicare for drug abuse treatment and equal the estimated expenditures under Medicaid. To control costs, the CHAMPUS program is currently evaluating the use of case-management and utilization review for the treatment of substance abuse.

Public insurance also differs from private insurance in terms of the level of cost sharing that is required. Whereas many private plans impose higher cost sharing for drug abuse treatment than for other types of medical care (particularly in the outpatient setting), public programs do not have differential cost sharing. Since increased cost sharing results in a decreased probability of seeking care, this is another desirable feature of public insurance programs. The level of cost sharing in public programs is also less than in private plans. This is particularly true of Medicaid, where cost sharing is required to be nominal.

Public Payment Mechanisms

Although benefits to public beneficiaries may be adequate, access to care can be limited because of the level of payments made to providers. This is particularly true of the Medicaid program and payments for physician visits. For instance, in Michigan, New York, and California (three states with large Medicaid programs), for a brief followup visit by a specialist, Medicaid pays only approximately one-third of the maximum allowable payment under the Medicare program (CRS, 1988). Since the actual fees charged by physicians may be higher than the maximum allowable under Medicare, the ratio of Medicaid payments to physicians' actual fees may even be lower than one-third. Physician participation in Medicaid is a function of payment levels and varies by specialty. Participation rates are particularly low for psychiatrists, the specialists most likely to be treating drug abusers. According to a study by Mitchell and Schurman, 42.2 percent of psychiatrists would not accept Medicaid patients[11] (Mitchell and Schurman, 1984). Medicare also uses a fee schedule for physician payments, but this schedule is considerably more reflective of physician charges. The CHAMPUS program pays physicians' actual charges. Under both of these programs, access to care because of inadequacy of payments is much less of an issue.

For hospitals, access to care may also be affected by reimbursement levels. Before fiscal year 1982, Medicaid was required to pay hospitals on the basis of reasonable costs. The Omnibus Reconciliation Act (OBRA) of 1981 changed the

---

[11]Based on HCFA/NORC physician surveys, 1977-78.

rules and now Medicaid is required to provide only hospital reimbursements that are adequate to meet the costs in an efficiently run hospital and provide reasonable access to care to beneficiaries (CFR 447.253). These amounts may be considerably less than actual costs and will thus affect the willingness of hospitals to accept Medicaid patients. Hospitals are under no obligation to accept Medicaid patients except for medical stabilization in the case of emergencies.[12] Thus, low payment levels provided under Medicaid will also affect access to hospital care.

CHAMPUS and Medicare both use a system of diagnosis-related groups to pay hospitals.[13] Since these rates are set to reflect the average costs of treatment across all hospitals, payments are generally adequate. Medicare has five different diagnosis-related groups for substance abuse. CHAMPUS has six. In CHAMPUS, the most frequent DRG was split into two because it was discovered that adolescents (specifically, persons under the age of 21) had significantly longer and more expensive hospital stays than adults (Zwanziger et al., 1992). Since adolescents are not part of the Medicare population, this fact was not noticed in the setting of the Medicare DRGs.

In summary, then, the presence of insurance benefits alone is not sufficient to assure access to needed treatment services. Adequate levels of payment to providers are necessary as well. Although this is less of an issue for CHAMPUS and Medicare, it is likely to be a very important one for Medicaid, where payment levels are generally low.

---

[12]Certain types of facilities, such as those constructed with federal grants under the Hill-Burton Act, must participate in Medicaid.

[13]Psychiatric hospitals and patients in psychiatric units of general hospitals are paid on a per diem basis.

4. Implications for Policy

Regulation of Private Insurance

The availability and types of benefits provided by employers can be influenced by both state and federal governments. The ability of the government to mandate drug abuse treatment benefits in the private sector allows for a redistribution of costs from the public sector to the private sector. Certain patients, who would previously have sought treatment from the public sector, may now seek care from private providers. In addition, by mandating the availability of drug abuse treatment benefits, the government can increase the overall amount of treatment services sought and provided.

Currently, 21 states and the District of Columbia have legislation mandating drug abuse treatment benefits (Thacker, 1988). State mandates apply to all employer-provided health insurance, except for plans offered by self-insured employers. The federal government regulates the health benefits provided by self-insured employers. Federal regulations are considerably less burdensome than state regulations. Therefore, large employers generally self-insure to create lower costs to the firm. Eighty-five percent of firms with over 1,000 employees self-insure; only 15 percent with fewer than 100 employees do so.

State mandates may take the form of either mandated availability of drug treatment benefits or a mandated minimum benefit package. As indicated in Figure 5, eight states simply mandate the availability of drug treatment benefits. Employers are free to choose the levels and types of benefits provided by their health plans. Thirteen states have mandated minimum benefit packages. For instance, New York has a mandated minimum benefit package for outpatient care and mandated availability for inpatient care. This applies to both alcohol and drug abuse treatment. On the inpatient side, 7 days of detoxification and 30 days of rehabilitation at approved facilities must be included as a minimum on all policies that cover inpatient hospitalization. On the outpatient side, 60 visits for diagnosis and treatment must be provided; 20 of these can be used by family members. There is considerable variation in the level of benefits mandated by states.

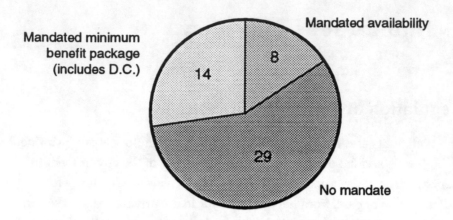

Figure 5—State Mandates for Drug Abuse Coverage

Employers, however, are currently faced with large, and ever-increasing health benefit costs for their employees. Mandated coverage for drug abuse might induce employers to drop other types of coverage. This may not be a socially desirable outcome.

At the federal level, proposals currently exist in Congress to provide for a mandated minimum health benefit package to be provided by employers that currently do not provide health insurance to their employees. The purpose of these proposals is to reduce the number of uninsured Americans, since the majority of the uninsured are the working poor. In 1987 there were 37 million uninsured, mostly comprising workers and their families (Short et al., 1989). Small employers are the least likely to provide health insurance, because of the high cost of health insurance. Thus, a minimum benefit package must not be too costly. Increasing the level of compensation will decrease the number of workers hired by such firms. In creating a package, tradeoffs between substance abuse coverage and other medical benefits must be weighed. At least one proposal does not contain any provision for outpatient drug abuse treatment or specialty inpatient care. Thus, it may be possible that drug abuse treatment benefits will not be part of such a requirement for minimum health benefits.

Expanding Drug Treatment Benefits Under Medicaid

Under current Medicaid guidelines, drug treatment benefits are not mandatory. Coverage for drug abuse varies considerably across states. Coverage for drug treatment provided by state Medicaid programs is currently not well understood (U.S. GAO, 1991), because only a limited number of services are mandatory under federal guidelines. In addition to mandatory services, states can elect to provide an optional set of services. Within both mandatory and optional service categories, states have considerable discretion in determining the scope, amount, and duration of services they will provide. If policymakers want the Medicaid program to uniformly provide treatment for drug abuse, then a specific provision for mandated coverage would have to be promulgated.

Federal guidelines require that states provide a certain set of mandatory medical services to categorically eligible recipients.[1] Mandatory services include inpatient hospital services other than services in an institution for mental disease, outpatient hospital services, laboratory and x-ray services, physician services, and early and periodic screening, diagnosis, and treatment (EPSDT) for persons under age 21. Medicaid programs can use the outpatient hospital setting to provide outpatient drug treatment if they choose. Not all outpatient treatment is necessarily covered, however. In California, for instance, only outpatient heroin detoxification is covered in this setting. On the inpatient side, Medicaid programs must provide all care that is medically necessary, irrespective of diagnosis. This means that any complicating medical condition will be treated as well as any detoxification that involves a life threatening condition. Medicaid programs do not have to provide for rehabilitation services, however, since these are generally psychosocial in nature and therefore not medically necessary.

States may also elect to provide a set of optional services in their Medicaid programs. Optional services relevant to the treatment of drug abuse include the clinic option and inpatient psychiatric hospital services for persons under age 21. The clinic option provides for care by a facility that is not part of a hospital but provides medical care on an outpatient basis. This option allows states to provide outpatient care in free-standing facilities. Whether a state with this option chooses to provide drug treatment in that setting is a policy decision made by the state. In 1987, 47 states and the District of Columbia had the clinic option (CRS, 1988). The inpatient psychiatric option allows states to provide treatment in an inpatient psychiatric hospital for adolescents. Medicaid does not permit coverage of care for persons between the ages of 22 and 65 in an institution for mental disease. For adolescents with severe psychological problems in addition to substance abuse, this option allows treatment in more specialized facilities. Again, this is an option that states may or may not choose. In 1987, only 36 states and the District of Columbia had the inpatient psychiatric option for persons under age 21.

---

[1]States may offer more restricted packages to medically needy eligibles.

Of equal importance with covered services, however, are treatments that federal guidelines specifically do not allow states to provide under their Medicaid programs. These relate primarily to the settings in which treatment for drug abuse can occur. Two specific provisions in the Medicaid statutes have significant implications for the delivery of medical services in the treatment of drug abuse. The first of these is that treatment in residential settings cannot be paid for under Medicaid. The second is that medical care for adults under the age of 65 cannot be provided in institutions for mental disease. Since drug abuse is classified as a mental disease in the international classification of diseases, this excludes care provided in facilities that specialize in the treatment of substance abuse.

The Medicaid regulations provide for inpatient care only in medical facilities. This includes inpatient hospitals, skilled nursing facilities, and intermediate care facilities. It does not include residential treatment facilities, an important setting for drug abuse treatment. Specifically, Medicaid will not pay for room and board charges in these facilities, which constitute the majority of the costs associated with treatment in this setting. It will pay for any medical services such as physician fees provided to persons under age 21 and over 65. It will also pay for medical services to those age 22–64 as long as the facility does not meet the definition of an institution for mental disease, which is unlikely, as discussed below. If Medicaid is to be used to pay for the treatment of drug abuse services, then this exclusion must change. Currently, inpatient care is available only in the acute hospital care setting. This is the most expensive setting in which treatment can occur. Aside from medically necessary detoxification, the majority of drug treatment consists of rehabilitation. These psychosocial services can be provided in other, nonmedical, settings, at considerably lower costs. Hospitals have large overheads because of the wide array of medical services they make available, and such an expensive setting is not warranted for the rehabilitative phase of drug abuse treatment. Detoxification usually lasts several days, whereas rehabilitation can last considerably longer. The standard inpatient treatment package for substance abuse is a 28-day stay, with up to 7 days of detoxification and 21 days of rehabilitation. Thus, three-quarters of the standard treatment regimen consists of rehabilitative services. This phase of treatment could be provided in residential settings at considerably lower cost. Although Medicaid does not cover drug abuse treatment in residential settings, Michigan (as mentioned above) does provide residential treatment to some Medicaid eligibles. It does not receive matching federal funds for this care, but the savings from the lower cost outweigh that loss. Since funds are entirely drawn from the state, a limited amount of residential care is available, however.

Even if Medicaid were to extend coverage to residential treatment facilities, treatment of adults in these settings would generally not be possible because of a second exclusion in the Medicaid regulations. Medicaid will not pay for any care received by persons aged 22–64 in an institution for mental disease which is defined as an institution with more than 16 beds "that is primarily engaged in providing diagnosis, treatment or care of persons with mental diseases, including medical attention, nursing care and related services" 42 CFR Sec. 435.1009 (1989).

Classification as an IMD is determined not by its licensure as such but by the overall character of the facility. The IMD exclusion has several important implications for drug abuse treatment. The first is that even if residential treatment facilities were permitted under Medicaid, care for adults in those facilities would likely still not be provided. Any residential treatment center would probably be classified as an institution for mental disease, since it is primarily engaged in the treatment of persons with substance abuse problems. Since substance abuse is classified as a mental illness, these facilities would fall under the IMD exclusion. Although the IMD exclusion might be waived for drug abuse facilities, this is unlikely to happen, since other facilities, such as those treating alcoholics, would have equally valid demands for an exclusion. The second implication of the IMD exclusion is that inpatient care for the drug abuse treatment of adults cannot take place in psychiatric hospitals or in hospitals specializing in substance abuse. The only setting in which inpatient care can be provided is the general acute care setting. This may not be the most appropriate setting for care in all cases, particularly for patients with mental problems as well as drug abuse problems. For adolescents, care can be provided in a psychiatric hospital but only if a state elects the inpatient psychiatric option for persons under the age of 21. A few states have elected this option.

Providing for care in residential settings would require allowing services to be provided in these facilities and relaxing the IMD exclusion. Whether this is feasible will depend on the fiscal implications to states and the federal government. Allowing care to be provided in these settings should result in substitution of expensive hospital inpatient care for less expensive residential care among states covering inpatient hospital care, thereby generating savings. It would also increase the demand for inpatient care overall if states not providing inpatient coverage decided to provide this benefit. Although this is desirable in that more treatment services will be made available, it will also increase overall costs to state programs. This may be mitigated somewhat by an offsetting decrease in expenditures in state-run facilities, however.

Drug abuse treatment is embedded in the broader world of mental health services delivery. Providing for care in residential settings and relaxing the IMD exclusion for drug abuse would also mean that these changes would have to be made for all mental health care. The fiscal implications of this type of change would be quite large. As indicated by the IMD exclusion, the federal government has not been willing to pay for specialty inpatient mental health care for persons other than the aged and children under Medicaid. It is unlikely to be willing to make such a large change to the Medicaid program. These are further barriers in the mainstreaming of public treatment financing away from block grants and toward Medicaid, advocated in the influential study by the Institute of Medicine (Gerstein and Harwood, 1990).

Eligibility Constraints for Drug Treatment Under Medicaid

There are considerable institutional barriers to changing eligibility requirements to Medicaid in such a way as to increase the number of drug abusers that are eligible. Since eligibility for Medicaid is directly linked to eligibility for AFDC and SSI, not all low-income persons are eligible for Medicaid. Persons must not only be poor, but they must also be either aged, disabled, blind, or in families with dependent children.[2] Based on information in the Current Population Survey, it is estimated that only about 41 percent of the poor (13.2 million) were covered by Medicaid during 1986 (CRS, 1988). Certain population groups are generally not eligible for Medicaid. They include nonelderly single persons (except pregnant women), childless couples, and most two-parent couples. Thus, single women or women in two-parent families who abuse drugs are unlikely to have coverage. Another group particularly likely to be ineligible for Medicaid but with high rates of drug abuse are males between the ages of 22 and 64. The Institute of Medicine (Gerstein and Harwood, 1990) has advocated the mainstreaming of public financing for drug abuse treatment away from block grants and toward Medicaid.

As policymakers turn to the Medicaid program as a possible source of funding for the treatment of drug abuse for low-income persons, however, it is clear that the program can serve only a subset of the needy population. To provide universal coverage for drug abuse treatment to all low-income persons, the

---

[2]Pregnant women and children under age 7 are also covered. Note that states may also choose to extend coverage to medically needy eligibles. These are persons who would otherwise qualify for AFDC or SSI, but whose income exceeds the categorically needy program standard, but not a separately defined medically needy standard. Alternatively, their income may exceed the medically needy standard but falls below it once medical expenses are subtracted. Medicaid must provide coverage for all categorically needy eligibles, but states have the option of including medically needy eligibles.

eligibility rules for Medicaid would have to be changed. If Medicaid eligibility were extended to all low-income persons, the costs of the Medicaid program to both the federal and state governments would increase tremendously. They would have to provide treatment not only for drug abuse but for the whole array of medical services provided under Medicaid for these newly eligible persons. The fiscal implications are so large that this is unlikely to be a feasible option. Currently, many states are facing budgetary problems. Since expenditures for Medicaid are a large component of state budgets, any large expansion in the program is unlikely to occur.

Without the ability to provide universal coverage, Medicaid could target certain population groups for increased access to drug abuse treatment services. One important population is pregnant women. Currently, treatment for drug abuse is not necessarily provided under state Medicaid programs. Medicaid benefits could be extended to provide treatment for drug abuse. Since the Medicaid program has responsibility for the medical care of the infants born to these women, this extension would be particularly advisable. The Institute of Medicine estimates that 105,000 pregnant women need drug treatment annually (Gerstein and Harwood, 1990). Children of addicted mothers are at high risk for low birthweight. Low birthweight infants generally have much higher health costs than normal birthweight infants (OTA, 1987). A General Accounting Office report found that drug-exposed infants were more likely than others to have a greater range of medical problems. Drug-exposed infants had hospital costs up to four times greater than did infants not exposed to drugs (U.S. GAO, 1990). Thus, treatment of drug abuse would be beneficial not only to the mothers but to their infants as well, and would probably result in overall savings to the Medicaid program.

Efforts in this direction may be hampered, however, by the lack of available treatment programs for pregnant women. Among programs that provide care to pregnant women, waiting lists are generally long. An illustrative example is a treatment program in Boston that received 450 calls for treatment during a given month. Because of waiting times, half the callers never called back and only 150 were eventually treated by that program (GAO, 1990). Other programs systematically deny treatment to pregnant women, in part because of legal concerns. A survey conducted of 78 drug treatment programs in New York found that over half of them denied treatment to pregnant women (GAO, 1990).

Summary

Policymakers can affect the amount of treatment services received for drug abuse in several ways. The first of these is regulation of insurance provided in the private sector. The government can mandate the presence as well as the types of benefits provided by private insurers. By mandating the presence of benefits for drug treatment, demand from private patients will increase because of the lower out-of-pocket costs. Not only will the overall demand for treatment rise, but certain patients, who might otherwise have depended on the public system of care, may seek treatment in the private sector. This would redistribute costs from the public sector to the private sector. Both state and federal governments can play an important role in the regulation of the private sector.

The amount of treatment services received in the public sector can be affected by policymakers as well. This can be achieved through a number of mechanisms, most obviously by increasing the direct support for treatment through such funding sources as block grants. This would increase the number of public treatment slots. Alternatively, increased access to insurance and better insurance benefits under Medicaid would have to be provided. The latter option would create more treatment on demand for public clients. Again, both the state and federal governments play key, and often intertwining, roles in any such changes. Funding for block grants is provided by the federal government, but these funds are administered by the states. The states themselves also provide direct funding for drug abuse treatment. On the insurance side, the federal government sets the eligibility and benefit guidelines for Medicaid but these are interpreted, and often modified, by the states. Currently, there are no explicit requirements to provide drug abuse treatment. In the absence of such a requirement, states interpret the benefit guidelines idiosyncratically. California provides very little drug treatment; Michigan has relatively generous benefits. The federal government specifically excludes care in certain types of facilities, most notably in residential treatment facilities. Among inpatient settings, these are the least costly. Michigan does provide care in residential treatment facilities under its Medicaid program, thereby forgoing the federal share (50 percent) of treatment costs for these patients.

Although federal guidelines currently exclude most of the drug abusing population, certain states, such as Michigan, have expanded eligibility guidelines to cover a greater portion of the poor population. States forgo the federal share of treatment costs for these individuals. Insurance coverage for a greater number of poor persons is available, however.

At the federal level, any changes to Medicaid increase federal outlays by only a fraction of the costs. Changes in direct dollars provided cost the federal government the entire amount. Under Medicaid, the federal government shares costs with the states at a fraction that is inversely related to the ratio of state per capita income to the national per capita income. States with low per capita incomes have higher federal shares. The federal share is a minimum of 50 percent. States therefore bear a substantial portion of the costs of their Medicaid programs, which in turn affects the types and scope of services they are willing to provide. From the federal perspective, however, this creates incentives to increase funding through Medicaid rather than through the provision of direct treatment dollars. Considerable institutional barriers exist, however, to increasing eligibility and treatment benefits under Medicaid.

Thus, both state and federal governments have important roles in the formulation of policy toward drug abuse treatment. These roles are not only complementary but often interconnected through existing institutional arrangements.

Appendix A
Medicaid

The public program that has received the most attention in terms of its potential for paying for the treatment needs of drug abusers is the Medicaid program. Created in 1965 as an amendment to the Social Security Act (Title XIX), Medicaid was intended to provide for the health care needs of certain categories of low-income persons.[1]

Eligibility

Eligibility for Medicaid is directly linked to the welfare system and to the Aid for Families with Dependent Children (AFDC) and Supplemental Security Income (SSI) programs in particular. States must provide Medicaid coverage to all persons receiving cash assistance under the AFDC program and most persons eligible for assistance under the SSI program. SSI is a program designed to provide cash assistance to the aged, blind, and disabled. The AFDC program provides assistance to families with children in which one parent is absent, incapacitated, or dead.

Pregnant women who meet the low-income standard are also eligible for Medicaid. Children born to Medicaid eligible women are also eligible for Medicaid.[2] States are required to provide services related only to pregnancy for pregnant women. For children, they must provide all services available to other AFDC eligibles. Finally, states must provide coverage for young children[3] who would otherwise be eligible for AFDC but who do not meet the definitions of a dependent child (for instance, one parent is not absent from the home). This provides expanded eligibility for poor children.

Persons qualifying for Medicaid because of eligibility for AFDC or SSI are known as categorically needy eligibles. States must extend Medicaid coverage to these

---

[1]The description of the Medicaid program provided here is for benefits in place in 1990.

[2]They are eligible for one year as long as the mother remains eligible and the child remains in the same household.

[3]All children under age 7 born after September 30, 1983.

groups.[4] States may also choose to provide coverage to medically needy eligibles. These are persons who would otherwise qualify for AFDC or SSI but whose income exceeds the categorically needy program standard, but not a separately defined medically needy standard. Alternatively, their income may exceed the medically needy standard but falls below it once medical expenses are subtracted. As of June 1987, 36 states (including the District of Columbia) covered medically needy eligibles (CRS, 1988). Finally, states may choose to extend Medicaid eligibility to groups not covered under federal guidelines. For instance, persons eligible for general assistance under a statewide program may be covered. For these persons, there are no federal matching dollars. States thus assume the entire financial responsibility for their medical care.

States have considerable flexibility in determining the income levels for welfare eligibility. They therefore also control the income levels required for Medicaid eligibility. This means that persons with identical financial circumstances would not receive the same treatment across states. In one state, they might be categorically eligible, in another only medically eligible, and in another state not eligible for Medicaid at all.

Types of Medical Services Covered Under Medicaid

Increasing eligibility for Medicaid is only half the challenge of providing increased access to drug treatment services. Of equal importance is the fact that the types of treatment for drug abuse vary considerably across states, because only a limited number of services are mandatory under federal guidelines. In addition to mandatory services, states can elect to provide an optional set of services. Within both mandatory and optional service categories, states have considerable discretion in determining the scope, amount, and duration of services they will provide. If policymakers want the Medicaid program to uniformly provide treatment for drug abuse, then a specific provision for mandated coverage would have to be promulgated.

Federal guidelines require that states provide a certain set of mandatory medical services to categorically eligible recipients.[5] Mandatory services include inpatient hospital services other than services in an institution for mental disease, outpatient hospital services, laboratory and x-ray services, physician services, and early and periodic screening, diagnosis, and treatment (EPSDT) for persons

---

[4]Whereas all persons receiving AFDC must be covered, states may apply more restrictive criteria than federal standards to SSI recipients

[5]States may offer more restricted packages to medically needy eligibles.

under age 21. EPSDT is designed to provide for "screening and diagnostic services to determine physical or mental defects in recipients under age 21" and "health care, treatment and other measures to correct or ameliorate any defects or chronic conditions discovered" 42 CFR Sec. 440.40 (1989).

Medicaid programs can use the outpatient hospital setting to provide outpatient drug treatment if they choose. Not all outpatient treatment is necessarily covered, however. In California, for instance, only outpatient heroin detoxification is covered in this setting. On the inpatient side, Medicaid programs must provide all care that is medically necessary, irrespective of diagnosis. This means that any complicating medical condition will be treated as well as any detoxification that involves a lifethreatening condition. Medicaid programs do not have to provide for rehabilitation services, however, since these are generally psychosocial in nature and therefore not medically necessary.

States may also elect to provide a set of optional services in their Medicaid programs. Optional services relevant to the treatment of drug abuse include the clinic option and inpatient psychiatric hospital services for persons under age 21. The clinic option provides for care by a facility that is not part of a hospital but provides medical care on an outpatient basis. This option allows states to provide outpatient care in free-standing facilities. Whether a state with this option chooses to provide drug treatment in that setting is a policy decision made by the state. In 1987, 47 states and the District of Columbia had the clinic option (CRS, 1988). The inpatient psychiatric option allows states to provide treatment in an inpatient psychiatric hospital for adolescents. Medicaid does not permit coverage of care for persons between the ages of 22 and 65 in an institution for mental disease. For adolescents with severe psychological problems in addition to substance abuse, this option allows treatment in certain more specialized facilities. Again, this is an option that states may or may not choose. In 1987, only 36 states and the District of Columbia had the inpatient psychiatric option for persons under 21.

The California Medicaid Program

Although each state has a different Medicaid program, for illustrative purposes the drug abuse benefits provided under the California program are presented here. California has the largest Medicaid program in terms of the number of beneficiaries and is the second largest in terms of expenditures.[6] California also has a large number of drug abusers. According to the 1987 NDATUS survey, California has the second largest number of persons in treatment for drug abuse; New York has the largest.

The California Medicaid program, known as MediCal, provides for limited treatment of drug abuse. Inpatient services are available only in the acute inpatient hospital setting and they are limited to treatment that is medically necessary. Thus, medically necessary detoxification will be provided along with treatment for any medical complications arising as a result of, or concomittant with, the drug abuse. Rehabilitation is not covered in the inpatient setting. The state also implements stringent utilization review of hospital admissions, which includes preservice authorization: Prior authorization must be obtained for any hospitalization. It is generally viewed that hospitalization for drug abuse treatment is not necessary unless there is a complicating medical condition or the situation is life threatening.

Outpatient care is also covered, but only for heroin detoxification. There is a limit of 21 days per episode for this type of care. The average number of days in detoxification per episode for clients of the Department of Alcohol and Drug Programs is 14,[7] thus this benefit seems fairly generous compared to actual use patterns. The average number of days in maintenance, however, is 385. Methodone maintenance is available only through an interagency agreement with the Department of Alcohol and Drug Programs, which administers publicly run treatment programs.

Several outpatient treatments may be covered through this interagency agreement. The existence of such treatment benefits depends on whether individual counties choose to participate in the agreement. Four types of outpatient treatments are covered under the agreement: (1) outpatient methodone maintenance, (2) outpatient drug-free treatment, (3) outpatient naltrexone treatment, and (4) day care habilitative. The latter is an outpatient drug-free program aimed at pregnant women. It is more intensive than the outpatient drug-free treatment.

Under the agreement, each county decides how much of its state general funds to put up for a federal match. It then receives an equal amount of federal dollars

---

[6]In 1986, California accounted for 15 percent of Medicaid recipients nationwide, a total of 3.5 million beneficiaries (CRS, 1988). In 1986, state Medicaid expenditures were 4.4 billion or 11 percent of Medicaid expenditures nationwide.

[7]These unpublished data were provided by the California Department of Alcohol and Drug Programs.

through Medicaid. By using this interagency agreement, the state pays for only half of the costs of treatment. The total amount of care that can be provided under this agreement is limited, however. Counties' participation in the interagency agreement is voluntary. Counties are free to choose which, if any, of the above treatments they will provide under the agreement. In certain counties, the four treatments described above may not be available. In others, only a subset are available. There are no limits on the number of episodes for which treatment can be provided or on the number of vists per episode. Subject to availability, beneficiaries can receive as much treatment as necessary. This is in sharp contrast to most private insurance where there are few limitations on the types of treatment that can be sought, but yearly or lifetime limits exist on the amount of care that can be received. It also contrasts with the CHAMPUS program (alcohol benefit), under which all types of treatments are covered, but only three drug abuse treatment episodes per lifetime are allowed.

In summary, under the California Medicaid program, treatment services for drug abuse are quite limited and services available to Medicaid beneficiaries vary by county. Inpatient treatments are limited to those that involve a complicating medical condition or a life-threatening situation. This essentially excludes inpatient rehabilitation and most inpatient detoxification. Inpatient treatment is not available in residential facilities. On the outpatient side, only heroin detoxification is available. Other outpatient treatments may be accessed through an interagency agreement, but these treatments vary by county. Aside from heroin detoxification, which has a limit of 21 days per treatment episode, there are no limits on the number of episodes for which treatment can be sought or for the number of visits per episode.

Appendix B
Medicare

The Medicare program is a program of public insurance intended to provide for the health care needs of the elderly and certain disabled persons. Since the majority of drug abusers are young and the disabled are a relatively small fraction of Medicare beneficiaries, Medicare expenditures for the treatment of drug abuse are small.

Drug abuse accounts for only a small fraction of Medicare dollars. According to Lave and Goldman (1990), in fiscal year 1987, total payments under the hospital part of Medicare (Part A) were $49.8 billion. Of this amount, $1.9 billion was spent on alcohol/drug abuse and mental health. Substance abuse cases (including both drugs and alcohol)[1] accounted for $201 million. Thus, only 11 percent of inpatient mental health dollars are spent on substance abuse, and mental health dollars themselves are only 4 percent of total inpatient dollars. Substance abuse therefore accounts for only one-half of one percent of Part A expenditures.[2] Expenditures on outpatient and physician services (Part B of Medicare) were also small. Total Part B expenditures were $29.9 billion, of which only $253 million was spent on alcohol/drug and mental health, 0.8 percent of the total. Since this includes both mental health and abuse of drugs and alcohol, the fraction attributable to drug abuse is even smaller.

The structure of benefits under the Medicare program, however, is of interest nonetheless, since Medicare is the largest third-party public insurer.[3] In 1987, total Medicare benefit payments were $81.2 billion (HCFA, 1989). Benefits for drug abuse treatment under Medicare are generous compared to other public types of insurance. Treatment for drug abuse in the inpatient hospital setting includes both detoxification and rehabilitation, as contrasted to Medicaid in which states may elect to provide only medically necessary detoxification and treatment of life-threatening conditions. There are no limits on the number of episodes of inpatient treatment that can be received by a beneficiary in contrast

---

[1]DRGs 433–438 (alcohol/drug use except toxic effects).

[2]Part A does include care in settings such as skilled nursing facilities and home health care where drug abuse treatment does not occur. Thus, substance abuse is a somewhat higher fraction of total Medicare hospital expenditures.

[3]The benefit descriptions provided here were effective in 1990.

to most private policies. On the outpatient side, there are no limits on the types of treatments that can be received, the number of episodes of treatment, or the number of visits per episode. This contrasts to Medicaid, in which the types of treatments provided may be quite limited, and to private policies, which tend to constrain the number of outpatient visits. As with Medicaid, however, inpatient care cannot be provided in residential treatment facilities. Benefits for care in psychiatric hospitals is also limited. Since the Medicare program is a national program, however, there is no variation in benefits across states or counties, as occurs with Medicaid.

Eligibility

Eligibility for Medicare, as with Medicaid, is limited to certain categories of individuals. There are two basic eligibility categories: the aged and the disabled. According to the 1987 NDATUS, only 0.5 percent of drug abusers in treatment are over the age of 65. Therefore, drug abuse treatment expenditures under Medicare are concentrated among the disabled. Among the disabled, those that are entitled to benefits under social security or the railroad retirement system are also eligible for Medicare.[4] Disabled persons not meeting these criteria may be eligible for Medicaid if they meet state criteria.[5] Disabled beneficiaries constitute approximately 10 percent of Medicare beneficiaries (HCFA, 1989). In 1987, there were 3 million disabled Medicare beneficiaries and 30 million aged.

Outpatient Care

Medicare coverage for outpatient care is generous compared to other types of insurance, such as Medicaid or private insurance. There are no limits on the number of episodes of treatments that may be sought or on the number of visits per episode. This contrasts markedly with private insurance in which limits are typically placed on the number of episodes for which treatment can be sought and on the number of visits that can be obtained per year. The lack of limitations on outpatient coverage for substance abuse is a result of a generous Medicare policy toward mental health in general. Medicare does not make any distinction in its benefits between substance abuse and mental health, in contrast to many private policies or CHAMPUS, which has more restrictive benefits for substance abuse than for mental health.

---

[4]Medicare coverage begins the 30th month after the first full calendar month of disability.

[5]Among the aged, all persons aged 65 and older who are entitled to social security or railroad retirement benefits are also eligible for Medicare.

Medicare has not always been so generous in its coverage of outpatient mental health and substance abuse treatment. Coverage for mental health has increased considerably over time. This is primarily in response to concerns that since such a small fraction of the Medicare dollar is spent on mental health, these services are underused by Medicare beneficiaries. Unlimited benefits only came into existence in 1990. Before 1988, Medicare would pay a maximum of only $250 for outpatient mental health care. This limit was raised to $450 in 1988 and to $1,100 in 1989. In 1989 Medicare also relaxed the limitations on outpatient care if a physician certified that without the care the beneficiary would be hospitalized. Finally, in 1990 all limits were eliminated for mental health care. This trend of increased benefits for outpatient treatment of mental health and substance abuse is in direct contrast to the private sector trend, which has been to increasingly limit benefits.

Although Medicare provides unlimited outpatient benefits for drug abuse treatment, it does mimic the private sector to the extent that the coinsurance rate for outpatient drug abuse treatment is higher than for other medical conditions. For medical conditions, the copayment rate for outpatient care is 20 percent. For mental health care, the copayment rate is 50 percent. This parallels copayment rates in the private sector. As already noted, the existence of differential copayment rates for drug abuse treatment tends to decrease the probability that drug abusers will seek treatment. This is particularly problematic for drug abuse treatment, since it is difficult for abusers to accept that they have a problem and need treatment. Adding financial disincentives decreases the probability that they will seek care. Fortunately for Medicare patients, however, they do not necessarily need to pay the increased copayment rate. If they receive their care from a provider that accepts assignment, then the lower copayment rate, 20 percent, applies. A provider who accepts assignment accepts the Medicare allowed charge as payment in full for services provided.[6]

In summary, Medicare outpatient benefits are quite generous compared to all other types of insurance. There are no limits on the number of visits per episode of care or on the number of episodes for which treatment is sought. Furthermore, Medicare patients can receive care from providers accepting assignment. They therefore have access to care for which their copayment rate is 20 percent, the same as for other medical conditions, and a far lower copayment rate than the typical private policy with a rate of 50 percent.

---

[6]Providers not accepting assignment may charge more than the Medicare allowed charge, leaving patients to pay not only the copayment rate but any excess of the charge over the Medicare payment level.

Inpatient Care

Medicare has fairly generous benefits for the inpatient treatment of drug abuse. Unlike some state Medicaid programs, Medicare will pay for both detoxification and rehabilitation. Further, unlike many private policies, there is no limit on the number of episodes of treatment that may be received. Medicare will pay for unlimited medically necessary inpatient hospital care[7] except for care in a psychiatric hospital (there is a limit of 190 days per lifetime of care in these types of facilities). Medicare will not, however, provide care in residential treatment facilities. Like Medicaid, all inpatient care is provided in the hospital setting.

Medicare controls the use of services and costs by placing limitations on providers. Use of inpatient care is influenced by utilization review mechanisms and a system of reimbursement for hospitals that pays them prospectively. Under Medicare, all cases of hospital care are reviewed retrospectively (after the care has taken place) to determine whether the care provided was medically necessary. Utilization review is done by Peer Review Organizations (PROs). These are groups of practicing doctors or other health care professionals who are paid by the federal government to review care provided to Medicare beneficiaries. Aside from determining whether the care provided was medically necessary, they also determine whether care was provided in the most appropriate setting and meets acceptable quality standards. Payment can be denied for any of these reasons. The provider, not the beneficiary, is at the risk of loss, however.[8] For substance abuse treatment, utilization review can be used to ensure that cases for which outpatient care was appropriate are not treated in the inpatient hospital setting, which is considerably more expensive.

The second method by which use of services is controlled on the provider side is by a method of payment that is prospectively based. That is, hospitals are paid a fixed amount in advance of providing treatment, irrespective of the actual costs of treatment. If costs are above the payment level then hospitals lose money, which gives them the incentive to be cost-effective. Naturally, the success of such a system depends on the adequacy of payments provided to hospitals. Payments are based on the diagnosis of the patient and certain characteristics of the hospital known to be related to costs.[9] Patient diagnoses are based on a set of 477

---

[7]The exception to this is that Medicare will not pay for any hospital care (for drug treatment or otherwise) if a beneficiary has exceeded 90 days in the hospital in a given benefit period and has run out of the lifetime reserve of days. This is unlikely to affect young persons abusing drugs.

[8]As long as the beneficiary could not have known that payment would be denied.

[9]Hospital characteristics include location (urban or rural), the level of local wages, teaching status, and presence of a patient population that consists of a disproportionate share of low-income patients.

DRGs. Each patient admitted is classified into one of these groups. Each DRG contains a base payment, which is then adjusted for various hospital characteristics to arrive at the final payment. The essential element of the system is that hospitals are paid in a manner that is disconnected from the actual costs of treatment but nonetheless provide adequate payments.

There are five substance abuse DRGs, listed below in Table B.1. Drug abuse and alcohol are combined in the definition of these groups. By extension, hospitals are paid the same amount whether a patient is abusing alcohol or drugs. The DRGs for substance abuse were revised several times before a final set was agreed upon. Until a final determination was made, substance abuse hospitals and substance abuse units in general hospitals were exempted from the prospective payment system, because it was argued that these specialized facilities would systematically lose money. As of October 1987, with the resolution of the definition of the substance abuse DRGs, these facilities were no longer exempted from the prospective payment system. Another set of hospitals remains exempt from prospective payment: psychiatric hospitals and psychiatric units in general hospitals. These facilities are still exempt from the prospective payment system because the existing DRGs and payment levels would result in systematic losses for these providers.[10] Drug abuse cases treated in these types of hospitals are not subject to the prospective payment system.

The basis of payment for each DRG is known as a weight that represents the relative costliness of treating a patient in that DRG. DRG weights are presented in Table B.2 along with the average lengths of stay for patients in each DRG.

Table B.1

DRGs for Substance Abuse Under Medicare

DRG	Description
433	Alcohol/drug abuse or dependence, left against medical advice
434	Alcohol/drug abuse or dependence, detoxification or other symptomatic treatment with comorbidities or complications
435	Alcohol/drug abuse or dependence, detoxification or other symptomatic treatment without comorbidities or complications
436	Alcohol/drug dependence with rehabilitation therapy
437	Alcohol/drug dependence, combined rehabilitation and detoxification therapy

---

[10]These hospitals are paid under the TEFRA (Tax Equity and Fiscal Responsibility Act) rules, which base payment on a target cost per case.

Table B.2

DRG Weights, Fiscal Year 1990

DRG	DRG Weight	Geometric Average Length of Stay	Outlier Threshold
433	0.3974	3.2	31
434	0.7886	5.7	34
435	0.5510	4.9	33
436	0.9873	12.0	40
437	1.2005	13.8	42

SOURCE: *Federal Register*, Vol. 54, No. 169, September 1, 1989.
NOTE: Effective for admissions on or after October 1, 1989.

Cost is directly related to the number of days.[11] The longest lengths of stay and therefore the highest costs occur in DRG 437, which includes both detoxification and rehabilitation. The second longest length of stay is in DRG 436, which includes only rehabilitation. Among the DRGs that include only detoxification (435, 436), the DRG with complicating medical conditions is the most expensive. The shortest lengths of stay are in the DRG for persons who left treatment against medical advice.

What is most striking in this table is that hospital lengths of stay for Medicare patients are considerably lower than the "standard" treatment package for substance abuse, provided by private insurers, which contains 7 days for detoxification and 21 for rehabilitation. The DRG with both detoxification and rehabilitation has an average length of stay of 14 days, well below the 28-day standard package. The rehabilitation-only DRG has an average length of stay of 12 days, again below the standard 21 days.[12] The number of days per hospitalization is implicitly limited by the DRG system, since it provides for a fixed number of dollars per stay. The implicit limits are well below 28 days.

For patients who are severely ill and require long stays, however, the system provides for additional payments, known as outlier payments. Hospitals receive an additional payment to the DRG payment for outlier cases to prevent large financial losses. There are two types of outliers, cost outliers and length of stay outliers. Payment depends on which type of outlier the case is. The Medicare outlier thresholds represent the length of stay that only 5 percent of cases exceed. What is of interest is that for the detoxification and rehabilitation DRG, the outlier threshold is 42 days, considerably more than 28 days. Thus, at least in the

---

[11]Average lengths of stay are measured by the geometric mean instead of the arithmetic mean, since the distribution of length of stay has a long right tail.

[12]Although incentives exist under the prospective payment system to decrease lengths of stay, such a large difference is unlikely to have been a result of PPS.

42

Medicare population, which is not representative of the population as a whole, the 28-day regimen does not seem to mirror actual use patterns.[13] In many cases it is longer than observed lengths of stay and in a small, but significant, number of cases it is much too short. This pattern also holds true in the CHAMPUS population, which is more representative of the overall U.S. population.

---

[13]Note that the Medicare DRG weights are based on both alcohol and drug abuse treatment. Alcoholism, however, is also treated under the 28-day regime.

Appendix C
CHAMPUS

Although CHAMPUS is a public insurance program, the eligibility criteria are quite restrictive, since they are linked to employment in the military. The CHAMPUS program provides health insurance for dependents of active duty military and for military retirees and their dependents. There are approximately 6 million CHAMPUS beneficiaries. Though small, the CHAMPUS program is nonetheless of interest because program expenditures for substance abuse and mental health care are quite high. In 1988, CHAMPUS expenditures for mental health accounted for approximately 25 percent of program expenditures. Drug abuse accounted for approximately 6 percent of mental health expenditures, or $32 million.[1]

Since drug abuse expenditures are so large, the benefit structures for treatment that have evolved under CHAMPUS are of interest.[2] The most notable feature of benefits for drug abuse treatment is that drug abuse may be treated either as a mental health condition with generous benefits or as an alcohol abuse problem with quite limited benefits. Which benefit structure holds depends on the existence of an alcohol abuse problem as a complicating condition. The alcohol benefit under CHAMPUS resembles benefits in the private sector for drug abuse treatment, with limitations on the number of episodes of treatment and on the amount of treatment services that can be obtained within each episode. The mental health benefit is quite generous and resembles benefits for drug abuse treatment under the Medicare program. Since drug abuse is a chronic recurring condition, benefits are considerably better under CHAMPUS when drug abuse is treated as a mental health problem than when it is treated as a substance abuse problem.

Eligibility

Eligibility for CHAMPUS is linked to employment in the military. Health care needs in this system are met not only by the private sector but by the system of

---

[1]Unpublished data from the CHAMPUS central office.
[2]The benefit descriptions provided here are those that were in effect in 1990.

military treatment facilities (MTFs). To gain an understanding of why CHAMPUS expenditures for mental health and substance abuse are so large, it is important to understand the interaction between these two systems. Active duty members receive all of their care in MTFs (except, possibly, emergency care). CHAMPUS covers dependents of active duty military and military retirees and their dependents. Eligibility for CHAMPUS ends at age 65 with Medicare eligibility. A large part of the care for active duty dependents and retirees and their dependents is provided through the system of MTFs. The CHAMPUS program is a system of health insurance designed to pay for care that cannot be obtained in these MTFs. CHAMPUS reimburses for civilian health services if inpatient care in appropriately located military hospitals is not available. For hospitalizations and pregnancy episodes, if the beneficiary lives close to an MTF then he or she must use that facility if space is available. For outpatient care, beneficiaries can use either MTFs or civilian providers. Care in the MTF is free, whereas care by civilian providers is subject to cost sharing according to CHAMPUS benefits. MTFs, however, have very limited capacity to provide mental health and substance abuse services. Therefore, disproportionately many of these services are sought in the civilian sector. The result is that mental health and substance abuse expenditures account for a disproportionately large fraction of CHAMPUS expenditures compared to other types of insurance. Because of generous benefits, this component of CHAMPUS expenditures has been rising over time and the CHAMPUS program is currently considering changing its benefits to contain costs.

Benefits for Drug Abuse Treatment

The benefits for drug abuse treatment fall into two categories: mental health and alcohol abuse. Which benefit structure applies depends on whether alcohol abuse is a complicating condition. The majority of drug abuse treatment occurs under the alcohol benefit. Under the mental health benefit, inpatient stays are limited to 60 inpatient days per year. There is no limit on outpatient visits.[3] Furthermore, there are no lifetime limits on the number of episodes of treatment that may be sought. This contrasts markedly with the alcohol benefit and with most private benefits, which are considerably more restrictive. Because of the chronic nature of drug abuse and the recurrent need for treatment, benefits are better suited to treatment needs when drug abuse is treated as a mental health problem.

---

[3]Treatments that involve more than two visits per week or more than 24 sessions in a calendar year must be approved under a utilization review agreement.

Under the alcohol benefit, coverage for treatment of drug abuse is considerably more limited. Only three episodes of treatment per lifetime are provided. In each benefit period,[4] limits on both inpatient and outpatient care apply. On the outpatient side, there is a limit of 60 outpatient visits and 15 family therapy visits per benefit period. Although less generous than the mental health benefit, this is still more generous than most private policies where the typical limitations on outpatient visits are 20 to 30 per year. On the inpatient side, up to 28 days of inpatient care are covered. This includes up to 7 days of detoxification and 21 days of rehabilitation, the standard inpatient treatment package for alcohol abuse. The 28 days of inpatient care also count against the 60 days of mental health care. Thus, a person having both a mental health problem and a drug abuse problem has less access to inpatient care than one with only a mental health problem. Whereas the 28-day limit is explicit in the benefit structure, there are also implicit limits imposed by the hospital payment system. Since CHAMPUS uses a prospective payment system for hospital care, based on DRGs the implicit limits on inpatient hospital care days may be lower. This will be discussed in more detail below.

As with all public insurance and a growing number of private policies, hospital inpatient treatment for drug abuse is subject to utilization review. CHAMPUS uses retrospective review. Cases are reviewed retrospectively for the necessity and appropriateness of care. If care is deemed unnecessary and payment is denied, then the beneficiary is at risk for the denied amount; this contrasts with the Medicare program, which also has retrospective review. Under Medicare, however, if payment is denied, the provider, not the beneficiary, is at risk for the denied amount.

Unlike Medicare and Medicaid, CHAMPUS will pay for inpatient care in alternative care settings. Specifically, CHAMPUS will pay for care in residential treatment facilities (RTCs). If inpatient care is sought in an RTC, then the same limitations apply as if hospital care was received, namely, a maximum of 28 days if alcohol abuse is a complicating condition and 60 days if it is not. CHAMPUS also has a separate benefit for adolescents under the age of 21, which provides for unlimited RTC care if medically necessary. There is no limit on the length of stay once the admission has been authorized. Admissions to RTCs are currently subject to both preadmission review and concurrent review. A primary reason for this is that the benefit is quite expensive to the program. In 1989, the CHAMPUS program expended approximately $110 million for RTC care. This provided for the RTC care of 3,000 adolescents. The average length of stay in

---

[4]Defined as the 365-day period that begins with the first day of rehabilitation.

1989 was 249 days with an average annual cost of $37,000.[5] Although these adolescents were primarily treated for mental illness, a substantial number had a secondary diagnosis of substance abuse.

Unlike many private policies, CHAMPUS does not have differential cost sharing for drug abuse treatment. For outpatient care, the copayment rate is 20 percent for dependents of active duty personnel and 25 percent for retirees and their dependents.[6] These copayment rates are less than the typical private policy where copayment rates of 50 percent for outpatient care are common. Therefore, under CHAMPUS financial disincentives to seeking treatment for drug abuse stemming from higher cost sharing do not exist.

Inpatient Payment Methodology

The CHAMPUS program pays prospectively for inpatient hospital care using DRGs. This system of payment is similar to that used by Medicare. The DRG system pays hospitals prospectively for a hospital stay based on the diagnosis of the patient. The prospective payment system for covered hospital services was implemented in October 1987. Substance abuse was initially exempted from the prospective payment system but is now included for care not occurring in a psychiatric hospital or the psychiatric unit of a general hospital. These are exempt from prospective payment because it was determined that they would systematically lose money under such a system. For care received in these specialized facilities, payment is made according to a hospital-specific per diem.

There are six DRGs for substance abuse under CHAMPUS and five under Medicare. The reason for this is that resource use in DRG 435, the most prevalent DRG for substance abuse, was found to vary significantly with age. Specifically, resource use was found to be much higher among adolescents than among adults (note that Medicare provides no differentiated coverage for adolescents). The CHAMPUS DRGs, therefore, split DRG 435 into two, one for patients under age 21 and one for those over age 21. The CHAMPUS DRGs are listed in Table C.1 and the DRG weights in Table C.2.

A study of DRGs for substance abuse under CHAMPUS (Zwanziger et al., 1992) showed that the DRG system discriminates poorly between substance abuse cases. The majority of cases fall into one DRG (DRG 435, which CHAMPUS has

---

[5]Unpublished data from the CHAMPUS central office.

[6]For care in free-standing facilities such as residential treatment facilities, cost sharing also follows the outpatient rules.

Table C.1

DRGs for Substance Abuse Under CHAMPUS

DRG	Description
433	Alcohol/drug abuse or dependence, left against medical advice
434	Alcohol/drug abuse or dependence, detoxification or other symptomatic treatment with comorbidities or complications
435	Does not exist; has been split into two DRGs 900 and 901
436	Alcohol/drug dependence with rehabilitation therapy
437	Alcohol/drug dependence, combined rehabilitation and detoxification therapy
900	Alcohol/drug abuse or dependence, detoxification, or other symptomatic treatment without comorbidities or complications, under age 21
901	Alcohol/drug abuse or dependence, detoxification, or other symptomatic treatment without comorbidities or complications, age 21 or over

Table C.2

DRG Weights for Substance Abuse Under CHAMPUS, Fiscal Year 1990

DRG	Weight	Arithmetic Average Length of Stay	Geometric Average Length of Stay	Long	Short
433	0.7875	8.5	5.5	33	1
434	1.1937	12.2	7.1	35	1
436	1.8675	25.2	23.1	51	5
437	1.6302	23.4	21.9	49	6
900	2.2317	25.2	18.4	46	1
901	1.3593	15.4	9.9	37	1

SOURCE: *Federal Register*, Vol. 54, No. 194, October 10, 1989.
NOTE: Effective for admissions on or after October 1, 1989.

split into 900 and 901).[7] The DRGs for substance abuse were only partially successful at classifying patients according to resource use. Only some of the differences in mean length of stay and mean charges across DRGs are significant in the CHAMPUS population.

Although the CHAMPUS program will pay for either 28 or 60 days per year for drug abuse treatment depending on whether alcohol abuse is a complicating condition, the DRG reimbursement rules actually imply that fewer days are covered. The DRG payment is set in such a way that it represents the average cost of treating a patient in that DRG across all hospitals that treat CHAMPUS substance abuse cases. Since the average lengths of stay are well below 28 days in all substance abuse DRGs, the actual number of days "covered" are

---

[7]Specifically, 66 percent of claims were in DRGs 900 and 901, 5.5 percent in DRG 433, 10.4 percent in DRG 434, 14.7 percent in DRG 436, and 3.4 percent in DRG 437.

considerably fewer. The average hospital will lose money if it keeps patients in the hospital much beyond the average length of stay in that DRG.[8] Thus, coverage for inpatient hospital care is actually considerably less than 28 days. The exception to this rule is hospitals that are not paid under the DRG system. Psychiatric hospitals and psychiatric units of general hospitals are exempt from prospective payment and are paid on the basis of a hospital-specific per diem.[9] Residential and free-standing facilities are paid according to billed charges. Since residential treatment facilities are also not paid on the basis of DRGs, the benefits provided by CHAMPUS do cover the full 28 or 60 inpatient days, whichever applies.

From Table C.2 we can see that the use of services is much higher among adolescents than among adults. The ratio of DRG weights for DRGs 900 and 901 is 1.65. Thus, it costs 1.65 times as much on average to treat a substance abuse patient under the age of 21 than over the age of 21. Adolescents have much longer lengths of stay, 25.2 days on average compared to 15.4 days for adults.[10] The data used to generate these numbers are for inpatient hospital care only. They do not include residential treatment facilities. Since CHAMPUS has an unlimited RTC benefit for adolescents, one would expect to see even longer lengths of stay in residential treatment facilities.

The lengths of stay in Table C.2 indicate that, on average, lengths of stay for inpatient hospital care are well below the standard 28-day treatment package provided by private insurers. The geometric mean length of stay for adolescents is 18.4 days and for adults 9.9 days.[11] Since the data used for this analysis were gathered before the introduction of the prospective payment system in CHAMPUS, these lengths of stay are not a result of the incentives created by PPS to decrease lengths of stay. Thus, we can be fairly confident that they represent

---

[8]The exception to this is if the patient becomes very costly. If the patient becomes either a cost outlier or a length of stay outlier, then the hospital receives an additional payment. If a case is a long stay outlier, that is it has a length of stay in excess of 3 standard deviations or 24 days, whichever is lower, above the geometric mean for that DRG, then the hospital receives the DRG payment plus 60 percent of the average daily rate for each covered day beyond the threshold. Cases can also be cost outliers. These are cases with standardized charges more than two times the DRG amount, or $27,000, whichever is greater. The hospital receives the DRG payment plus 80 percent of costs in excess of the threshold. Costs are defined as charges times a cost-to-charge ratio. If a case is both a cost outlier and a length of stay outlier, then the hospital receives the higher payment.

[9]Hospitals with more than 25 CHAMPUS mental health discharges per year are paid on a hospital-specific basis, those with less, on a regional average per diem. Cost per day does not vary with DRG or age, factors that have been shown to be related to daily costs. CHAMPUS uses the same list of exempt providers as Medicare.

[10]Note that these figures are for substance abuse and not specifically for drug abuse. The substance abuse DRGs do not differentiate between alcohol and drug abuse, thus these costs and lengths of stay are pooled across all types of substance abuse.

[11]The geometric mean is the appropriate measure of average length of stay as opposed to the arithmetic mean, because the distribution of lengths of stay has a long right tail.

actual use patterns. Conversely, the outlier thresholds indicate that a significant number of patients have considerably longer lengths of stay. For adolescents, the long stay outlier threshold is 46 days and for adults it is 37 days. For these cases, a 28-day treatment package is clearly insufficient to cover observed patterns of use. Again, given the benefit structure for inpatient substance abuse treatment, it cannot be argued that insurance benefits are driving these long lengths of stay. Cases included in the substance abuse DRGs are therefore for both alcohol and drug abuse. Alcohol abuse is paid under the alcohol benefit as are most cases of drug abuse. Thus, the vast majority of substance abuse cases are subject to the alcohol benefit, which limits inpatient care to three episodes of care per lifetime and 28 days of inpatient care per episode. Cases with stays in excess of 28 days before the introduction of PPS resulted in a loss of coverage beyond the 28th day. Since hospital care is extremely expensive, it is highly unlikely that physicians would have kept patients that long unless it was medically necessary.[12]

Zwanziger et al. (1992) found that on substance abuse DRGs under CHAMPUS, 13.9 percent of substance abuse discharges were long stay outliers. These cases accounted for 40 percent of inpatient days and total charges in DRG 435 (the most prevalent substance abuse DRG). For these cases, long hospitalizations were observed. Assuming that the CHAMPUS population is fairly representative of the employed population, or at least of their dependents, this means that private insurance, which often has stringent limits on the number of days of inpatient care provided per year, does not provide sufficient coverage for these cases.

Another finding of the Zwanziger study was that in 1988, approximately 20 percent of total discharges for substance abuse hospitalizations were for patients with more than one substance abuse admission. This is significant because it indicates that for certain parts of the drug abuse population, multiple hospitalizations in a given year are required. Yet, under the current CHAMPUS benefits, only one hospitalization is allowed per year. Many private policies also limit the yearly number of days in treatment to that of one standard treatment package, 28 days. Combined with the fact that on average lengths of stay are below 28 days but that for a small fraction of patients, presumably the most severely ill, lengths of stay are much higher, it seems that reimbursement based on one standard 28-day treatment does not correlate well with observed patterns of use. For the majority of patients, use of inpatient services is less than 28 days. For the most severely ill, who require either long lengths of stay or multiple

---

[12]Some of the long lengths of stay, however, may be due to drug abuse cases without alcohol abuse as a complicating condition. In that case, 60 days per year are provided as a benefit and even these long lengths of stay would be covered.

admissions, this does not provide enough coverage. Most private policies as well as the CHAMPUS alcohol benefit are based on this standard treatment regimen, offering only one treatment per year. Benefits for mental health conditions under CHAMPUS are more generous. Up to 60 days of inpatient care are provided per year and there is no limit on the number of episodes of treatment. When drug abuse is treated as a substance abuse problem, then only one 28-day inpatient stay is covered per year, and only three episodes are covered per lifetime. Since drug abuse is a chronic recurring condition, such reimbursement policies are likely to reduce access to needed care.

Bibliography

Aaron, Henry, and William Schwartz, *The Painful Prescription: Rationing Hospital Care*, The Brookings Institution, Washington, D.C., 1984.

Beschner, G., "The Problem of Adolescent Drug Abuse: An Introduction to Intervention Strategies," in A. Friedman and G. Beschner (eds.), *Treatment Services for Adolescent Substance Abusers*, National Institute on Drug Abuse, Department of Health and Human Services, DHHS Publication No. (ADM)85–1342, Washington, D.C., 1985.

Bureau of Labor Statistics, U.S. Department of Labor, *Employee Benefits in Medium and Large Firms, 1988*, Bulletin 2336, August 1989.

Bureau of Labor Statistics, U.S. Department of Labor, *Employee Benefits in State and Local Governments, 1987*, Bulletin 2309, May 1988.

Butynski, W., D. Canova, and S. Jensen, *State Resources and Services Related to Alcohol and Drug Abuse Problems, Fiscal Year 1988*, A Report for the National Association of State Alcohol and Drug Abuse Directors, Inc., Washington, D.C., June 1989.

Butynski, W., and D. Canova, *State Resources and Services Related to Alcohol and Drug Abuse Problems, Fiscal Year 1987: An Analysis of State Alcohol and Drug Abuse Profile Data*, A Report for the National Institute on Alcohol Abuse and Alcoholism and the National Institute on Drug Abuse, National Association of State Alcohol and Drug Abuse Directors, Inc., Washington, D.C., August 1988.

Congressional Research Service (CRS), *Medicaid Source Book: Background Data and Analysis*, A Report prepared by the Congressional Research Service for the Subcommittee on Health and the Environment of the Committee on Energy and Commerce, U.S. House of Representatives, 100th Congress, 2d Session, Committee Print 100-A, U.S. Government Printing Office, Washington, D.C., November 1988.

Foster Higgins, *Health Care Benefits Survey Findings*, A. Foster Higgins & Co., Inc., Princeton, New Jersey, 1988.

Foster Higgins, *Health Care Benefits Survey, 1988: Tables of Survey Responses*, A. Foster Higgins & Co., Inc., Princeton, New Jersey, 1988.

Gerstein, D., and H. Harwood (eds.), *Treating Drug Problems: A Study of the Evolution, Effectiveness, and Financing of Public and Private Drug Treatment Systems. Volume 1*, National Academy Press, Washington, D.C., 1990.

Health Care Financing Administration, Bureau of Data Management and Strategy, *1989 HCFA Statistics*, U.S. Department of Health and Human Services, HCFA Pub. No. 03294, Washington, D.C., September 1989.

Health Care Financing Administration, U.S. Department of Health and Human Services, *Health Care Financing Program Statistics: Medicare and Medicaid Data Book, 1988,* HCFA Publication No. 03270, Washington, D.C., April 1989.

Health Care Financing Administration, U.S. Department of Health and Human Services, *The Medicare Handbook, 1990,* HCFA Publication No. 10050, Washington, D.C., 1990.

Health Care Financing Adminstration, *State Medicaid Manual, Part 5: Early and Periodic Screening, Diagnosis, and Treatment (EPSDT),* Department of Health and Human Services, Health Care Financing Administration, HCFA Publication No. 45–5, Washington, D.C., 1990.

Kronson, Marc, "Substance Abuse Coverage Provided by Employer Medical Plans," *Monthly Labor Review,* April 1991.

Lave, J., and H. Goldman, "Medicare Financing for Mental Health Care," *Health Affairs,* Vol. 9, No. 1, Spring 1990, pp. 19–30.

Letsch, S., K. Levit, and D. Waldo, "Health Care Financing Trends," *Health Care Financing Review,* Vol. 10, No. 2, Winter 1988, pp. 109–122.

Levin, B. L., "State Mandates for Mental Health, Alcohol, and Substance Abuse Benefits: Implications for HMOs," *GHAA Journal,* Winter 1988, pp. 48–69.

Manning, W. G., et al., *Health Insurance and the Demand for Medical Care: Evidence from a Randomized Experiment,* RAND, R-3476-HHS, February 1988.

Mitchell, J., and R. Schurman, "Access to Private Obstetrics/Gynecology Services Under Medicaid," *Medical Care,* Vol. 22, No. 11, November 1984, pp. 1026–1037.

Office of National Drug Control Policy, *National Drug Control Strategy: Budget Summary,* The White House, Washington, D.C., January 1990.

National Institute on Drug Abuse and National Institute on Alcohol Abuse and Alcoholism, *National Drug and Alcoholism Treatment Unit Survey (NDATUS) 1987: Final Report,* DHHS Publication No. (ADM) 89–1626, U.S. Department of Health and Human Services, Public Health Service, Alcohol, Drug Abuse and Mental Health Administration, Rockville, Maryland, 1989.

National Institute on Drug Abuse (NIDA), *Demographic Characteristics and Patterns of Drug Use of Clients Admitted to Drug Abuse Treatment Programs in Selected States,* Department of Health and Human Services, Washington, D.C., 1985.

Office of National Drug Control Policy (ONDCP) White Paper, *Understanding Drug Treatment,* Washington, D.C., June 1990.

Office of Technology Assessment (OTA), *Neonatal Intensive Care for Low Birthweight Infants: Costs and Effectiveness,* Office of Technology Assessment, Congress of the United States, Washington, D.C., December 1987.

Short, P., A. Monheit, and K. Beauregard, *A Profile of Uninsured Americans*, National Medical Expenditure Survey Research Findings 1, National Center for Health Services Research and Health Care Technology Assessment, Department of Health and Human Services, DHHS Publication No. (PHS) 89–3443, Rockville, Maryland, September 1989.

Social Security Bulletin, *Annual Statistical Supplement, 1986*, U.S. Deparyment of Health and Human Services, Washington, D.C., December 1986.

Social Security Bulletin, *Annual Statistical Supplement, 1989*, U.S. Deparment of Health and Human Services, Washington, DC, December 1989.

Thacker, W., Director, Office of Substance Abuse Services, Commonwealth of Virginia, on behalf of NASADAD, "Insurance Coverage and Drug and Alcohol Abuse," Appendix 1, hearing before Senate Committee on Commerce, Consumer Protection and Competitiveness, Committee on Energy and Commerce, 100th Congress, 2nd Session, September 8, 1988.

U.S. Office of Personnel Management (OPM), *A Guide to Substance Abuse Treatment Benefits Under the Federal Employees Health Benefits Program For 1990*, Retirement and Insurance Group, Washington, D.C., November 1989.

U.S. General Accounting Office, *Substance Abuse Treatment: Medicaid Allows Some Services But Generally Limits Coverage*, GAO/HRD-91-92, June 13, 1991.

Zwanziger, J., et al., Prospective Payment for CHAMPUS Exempt Services: An Analysis of Children's Hospital, Substance Abuse, and Psychiatric Services, RAND, R-3700-HA, 1992.